SILVER

SILVER

Economic Inflation

To

Capital Gain

By

Major T. Beesley

Beesley Books Edition

Copyright © 2016 by Major Theodore Beesley

Major Publishing LLC

All rights reserved.

Printed in the United States of America

First Printing: June 2017

Book Description

There are loads of explanations for endowment in silver and there are numerous means to do so. Reliant on how lofty the price hike is, all the means could be redeemed over the sequence of the subsequent years. Silver ingot is as a stockpile of worth. Whenever price hike strikes, numerous resources will mislay genuine significance. Given that silver is valued universally in U.S. dollars, when price hike of the U.S. dollar causes its worth to drop comparative to other coinage, the price of silver, in U.S. dollars, will go up. Silver will cling to its usefulness in this worldwide financial system. The value of outlandish merchandise, and local commodities enclosing outlandish gears, will go up. Furthermore, it is as a great protection in opposition to price rises. If rise in price is comparatively easygoing, silver ingots will persevere with you even during a boom. Relative to total assets in the world, the current value of all the gold bullion in the world is tiny. Like-wise, the value of all the silver bullion in the world is tiny compared to that of gold bullion. If merely a solitary figure proportion of the wealth at present put in other resources, like bonds, stock exchange, and land holdings, is employed for massive purchase of valuable metals such as silver, the cost of the latter will go up much more rapidly than the tempo of tumefaction. At the same time as this comes about, loads of prospective gold financiers will be stunned by the value of gold and switch to endowment in silver as a substitute. Also, endowment in silver bullion is for indemnity opposed to monetary catastrophe.

Silver - an article of trade with more than a thousand industrialized applications and utilizations internationally is monetary indemnity.

I, Major Theodore Beesley - the author of this book will discuss ways and means to endow in silver which you can buy for a song so that you could be back on your feet as soon as possible.

Certainly, this book needs to be read!

Contents

Silver has a whole host of uses.

Value of silver will ultimately ape up, buy silver right away!

Why Silver coins can save your ass in the forthcoming times?

Finest choices of silver investments:

Every cloud has a silver lining!

Get Physical Silver now!

*I*ntroduction:

Silver in the shape of coins, bars, ingots or rounds have been bought and sold and substituted for treasured commodities all through olden times. These days it remains the tough component it has forever been. Fiat or paper currency that has been sanctioned by administrations in the course of pronouncement, cannot embrace their own in opposition to silver.

Paper currency can become valueless; silver will forever be a prized metal and will continue to have merit or value.

Silver in bulk is created in diverse shapes, but by a great amount, the most suitable is the silver coin. Silver is a stunning valued metal; getting hands on the tangible metal - besides a price hike approach can be gratifying and worthwhile. Silver has been bona fide currency for thousands of years and holding it helps emphasize the features that make it an ideal medium for transposition.

Immeasurable beneficiaries and shareholders are of the same opinion that any purchase of silver in the shape of coins harmonizes the expenses connected with minted legal tender. Need for silver has extended considerably during the previous many years owing to the worth of its characteristics which are as follows: Silver is tough, malleable, flashes on luminosity, puts forward incomparable thermal dynamism, is absolute in electrical applications, and can tolerate tremendous thermal readings. Several principals saving authorities forecast that silver is one of the most imperative merchandise in the world and purchasing silver is one of the supreme venture prospects for the upcoming. Momentous silver trade makes headway by those who are anxious about the threat of monetary inflation occurring at a very high rate. Resolute venture capitalists reflect on collecting ninety % silver coins that were issued prior to the year 1965 in values of ten cent coins, the George Washington quarters, and the Kennedy half-dollars. Above and beyond acquiring the low tariff cost for the biggest amount of silver, countless believe that it is essential for simplicity of use if the requirement for bargain crops up.

The worth of silver!

The hauling out of silver began approximately five thousand years back. Silver was initially extracted in around 3000 before the time of Jesus Christ, in Anatolia (Present-day Turkey.) These premature veins of metal ore in the earth were a costly reserve for the societies that thrived in the Modern Middle East, largest of the Greek islands and Greece during ancient times. In around 1200 before the time of Jesus Christ, the hub of silver creation reallocated to Lavrion of contemporary Greece on the Aegean Sea. There it sustained to nourish the mushrooming territories of the area. In approximately 100 Anno Domini, Spain became the capital of silver production. The Spanish excavations were the major supplier for the Roman Empire and an essential trading component along the Asian spice routes. With the Moorish incursion of Spain, the system of pulling out of silver drifted to a broader array of countries, nearly all of them in Central Europe. {It may not be out of place to mention here that the Moors were a wandering community from North Africa; initially they were the residents of Mauretania. When they marched into Spain, they took their religious convictions and customs with them, in 711.} Unearthing of more than a few main silver excavations took place amid 750-1200 A.D., counting Eastern Europe (Russia, Czech Republic, Croatia, Hungary, Moldova and so forth) and Germany. The five hundred year phase from 1000-1500 A.D. was one of momentous developments (as a result of an augmented number of collieries) in addition to up gradation in production and gadgets. On the other hand, no solitary episode in the bygone instances of silver opposes the value of the detection of the Americas in the year 1492. This meaningful discovery and the years that ensued re-discovered the position of silver all over the planet.

The Spanish take-over of the Americas showed the way to pulling out of silver, that spectacularly overshadowed no matter what had appeared previous to that time. Amid 1500 and 1800, Peru, Mexico and Bolivia materialized more than eighty-five percent of global creation and commerce. Afterward, quite a few other countries started to contribute Silver more noticeably, (chiefly the United States with the discovery of the Comstock Lode in Nevada----- a lode of silver ore placed under the eastern slant of Mount Davidson, a mountain in the Virginia Range in Nevada-------at that time western Utah Region). It was the earliest key discovery of silver ore in the United States. Silver creation sustained to spread out internationally, mounting from forty to eighty million troy ounces per annum by the eighteen seventies. The troy ounce is an entity of regal measure, now generally used to calculate the dimensions of costly metals. The phase from 1876 to 1920 symbolized an outburst in both technical modernization and utilization of novel areas globally. Creation over the very last section of the nineteenth centennial increased fourfold over the standard of the initial seventy-five years to a sum of almost one hundred and twenty million troy ounces per annum.

Likewise, latest breakthroughs in Europe, Australia and Central America significantly amplified entire creation of silver across the globe. The two decades amid the year nineteen hundred and nineteen twenty eventuated in a fifty percent amplification in worldwide creation, and fetched the sum to almost one hundred and ninety million troy ounces per annum.

These augmentations were prompted by unearthing in Africa, Canada, the United States, Japan, Mexico, Chile, and other states.

In the preceding centenary, innovative equipment and machinery have also played a role in a substantial increase in global silver creation. Most important steps forward take account of steam-assisted boring, excavation, reserve draining, and better transport. In addition, progresses in methods of pulling out enhanced the skill to detach silver from other metallic minerals and made it achievable to manage bigger quantities of raw material that held silver.

Such techniques were vital for the bigger quantities of manufacture, since several of the high-grade raw materials all over the globe had been mostly exhausted by the conclusion of the nineteenth centennial.

These days, over and above five thousand years (after antique societies initially started to excavate this expensive metal)

Main countries in universal silver mine creation from 2010 to 2015 (in metric tons)

This gauge offers a country-wise itemization of universal silver mine creation from 2010 to 2015.

	2010	2011	2012	2013	2014	2015 *
Mexico	4,410	4,150	5,360	4,860	5,000	5,400
China	3,500	3,700	3,900	4,100	4,060	4,100
Peru	3,640	3,410	3,480	3,670	3,780	3,800
Australia	1,860	1,730	1,730	1,840	1,720	1,700
Russia	1,150	1,350	1,500	1,720	1,330	1,500
Bolivia	1,260	1,210	1,210	1,290	1,340	1,300
Chile	1,280	1,290	1,190	1,170	1,570	1,600
Poland	1,180	1,170	1,150	1,200	1,260	1,300
United States	1,270	1,120	1,060	1,040	1,180	1,100
Canada	600	572	663	627	493	500

Why this costly metal is greater than any fiat currency?

Quite a few financial experts are suggesting the idea of taking up some type of a gold standard in the United States of America even if none have gone into any great schedule.

Reliable money also encourages necessity to imagine resourcefully as regards to becoming accustomed with money in the form of bills and coins.

The protracted olden times of gold and silver being used as capital going back to very old times even now carries some weight. The indispensable values behind reliable money are unchanging. The application of the knowledge and the usage of computers may make it effortless than ever for reserve banks to generate and maneuver digital money units.

To produce improvement or decline, economy based on digital computing technologies will carry on continuing living for a long time and will become accepted as normal. By and large, it can be for recuperation.

There is not anything innately fraudulent as regards to electronic transmission of commercial dealings on the internet or payments with smart phones, and there is no explanation why silver can't incorporate into these and upcoming systems.

Actually, the economy based on digital computing technologies spurs a globe of modernistic conveniences for open market unconventional cash to begin taking an effect. Unconventional money and unconventional banking supported eventually by substantial silver could signify the leading risk to the paper money system of the Central Bank of the United States.

Promoters of stable money should not be protected from applications of new techniques of ethics of stable money. In case we don't, subsequently our movement will be alleged as old-fashioned, and outmoded. Regardless of how securely we make the argument for the excellence of a currency supported by silver, if folks relate hard money absolutely with the times of yore, they won't distinguish it as indispensable or practical these days.

Any person who believes that hard currency necessitates the unswerving substitute of silver and gold coins right through the financial system is unequivocally mistaken. Even all through the peak of the U.S. gold standard system in the deferred nineteenth century, gold coins were more prone to be detained as investments than to be exhausted frankly in the financial system. Folks more frequently paid for deliverables using silver coins

or paper currency that were eventually redeemable
in gold.

Gold and silver can effortlessly be dealt with electronically:

It is likely that coins formulated from gold and silver never flow far and wide as transferrable coinage another time. They will carry on to be put aside (as investments) and stockpiled for employment (as currency throughout crisis) should the necessity crop up. There are benefits of being competent to trade gold and silver price in some way. Those of you who have at any time purchased a sack of ninety percent silver coins earlier than 1965 are well-acquainted with the fact that they can no longer be used on account of being damaged by continued use gradually progressively with time. It's not a hitch for depositors who purchase trash silver in large quantities by its whole silver content. However it can be a setback in dealings when a profoundly overused coin no more grasps its total essential value. (The Coinage Act or the mint act of 1792 described a buck as 371.25 grains of silver.)

Balance of a card for shopping without cash or a component of virtual currency associated with a particular amount of silver being positioned in a safe storage resolves that setback. It also elucidates the dilemma of usual financial credit balances being essentially valueless. Bit coin is eventually supported by nothing; whereas bank financial credit balances correspond to a signed document acknowledging a debt financed by nil but the unconditional guarantee by one entity to back the interest and principle of another entity's debt of the banks and U.S. administration. It is the conception of belief in a fundamental ability that is obsolete. Nowadays, practically no proficient experts in economy believe in a Soviet-made monetary system, the one in which the country or administration makes financial pronouncements rather than the communication between patrons and trades. However, although the Soviet Union disintegrated quite a few years back, its dishonored economic system replica carries on to the calendar day with reference to coinage and annual percentage of the loan outstanding.

Autonomous national establishments that carry out monetary policies are still being given the authority to place interest rates for the entire financial system, while they have ascertained to be inexpert at best (and frequently out-and-out incompetent) at predicting monetary successions and putting a stop to economic surges and closures in the market. Ever since the year 2009, the disparaging Central bank of the US has siphoned a very large amount of paper money into the payment scheme and Wall Street (a lane in lower Manhattan that is the fundamental abode of the New York Stock

Exchange and the ancient control center of the biggest U.S. brokerages and financial companies that provide various financial related and other services as well as those companies that buy and sell goods or assets for clients) carrying out a huge relocation of assets and placing the dollar's universal trustworthiness at jeopardy.

This hybrid monetary system includes:

- Some coinage, whose cost is not controlled by any particular system
- Several coins whose cost is decided by a mishmash of administrative intrusion and the market
- A few that are attached to one coinage or a collection of legal tender

Although this system would maintain the central bankers in authority yet will re-introduce gold as a restriction on their ability to escalate. While the

Steve Forbes proposal (according to which American contributors of tax are given a prospect to select effortlessness versus intricacy and a solitary rate over a great deal of subtractions of levy) is not an ultimate free-market financial system, yet it could operate as a representation for improving the subsisting system – and ultimately changeover to one that eliminates the Federal Reserve on the whole.

Putting a stop to the Federal Reserve Bank could signify instituting a modernist silver and gold benchmark (possibly by way of a Constitutional adjustment that attaches the worth of the U.S. dollar with regard to silver/gold. Or else a gold standard could be attained by denouncement of administration's control of coins or bank notes exclusively; and permitting acquisition of laissez faire economics currencies (a number of which may be exchangeable in valuable metals; while others may not be so).

Computerized gold and silver expenditure by means of novelties such as Bit Gold and the Gold Standard Society's Digital Gold 2.0 may demonstrate in the upcoming that free-market's globally traded currency (that can serve up as a dependable and unwavering store of worth) is practicable for every day transactions. All it will then require is the justification to contend openly with the U.S. dollar as money backed by administration.

Silver's operational value from 2000 to Middle 2014 in opposition to paper money or coins has not been jaded by any process. Silver has cherished a middling of 1973 percent and a mean worth of 307 percent alongside the paper money. The biggest unsuccessful paper money against silver has been the Congolese Franc. Silver has esteemed 84117 percent its initiation 2000 one ounce value in the Congolese Franc. Paper money that has temporized most gallantly to Silver are the Somali Shilling (-85 percent), the Swiss Franc (-118 percent), and the Czech Korna (-119 percent) in that order. So far in the twenty-first centennial, Silver has also exceeded valuable metal equivalents i.e. platinum and palladium; at the same time as somewhat performing less well than expected twenty-first centennial appraisal approval of gold.

*T*he silver bullet:

Contrasting money in the form of banknotes, expensive metals by themselves have significance. You simply necessitate walking away from the lane and shining a bit of silver and folks would obviously be fascinated by it. If you dump a bit of silver on the lane, there is a likelihood that it will disappear when you walk rearward to it. That's how authoritative the legendary task of silver is as a stockpile of worth; it is an assessment of worth.

The equivalent cannot be assumed regarding a lifeless bit of paper. The truth is that the fiat money is in essence inert bits of paper. The single-handed inscription on them that offers them worth is that there is an assurance by the administration that the bit of paper has worth. Just once folks evade faith in the administration supporting that paper; that bit of paper goes back to being a valueless bit of paper. The equivalent cannot be asserted about costly metals such as silver currency.

Silver as a protection against price hike:

It is specifically owing to the historical role of silver as a stockroom of worth (and its generally recognized power to amass value) that silver expresses as a great guard against price hike. Silver runs with hike. With each elapsing year as hike escalates and as currency becomes low-priced, valuable metals persevere with a point of time. They permit you to guard against hike in a similar way that land holdings approve of price hike.

Mechanized challenge of silver:

One more justification why silver will carry on having significance in the future is the reality that there is a tangible commercial necessity for it. There are plenty of mechanized stuff and goods that need silver. The latter is also considered necessary in numerous business progressions. If you gradually reduce its past position (as a pile up of worth or its use as personal ornaments) silver will nevertheless be in need! As a consequence, it will never lose value because there is an industrial demand for it.

Demand of silver-based ornaments:

All the way through history, folks have cherished to put on silver ornaments. There is an unspecified thing about silver's brilliant silvery radiance that makes folks attracted to it. In view of the fact that gold is very high-priced, folks frequently consider silver as a minor replacement for gold ornaments. Bearing in mind its lesser cost, a great many more individuals make use of silver ornaments. It is this recognition that guarantees that there is a customer demand for silver. Specifically similar to the previous discussion regarding the trade need for silver, the stipulation for silver continues in the course of time. Actually, in countless kingdoms, silver is chosen as an ornament. That's why silver coins are a distinguished asset and can be liquefied into their base metal parts and transformed into silver objects, whether for manufacturing intentions or in the form of ornaments. In a similar manner, commercial silver and ornaments can also be transformed into silver coins.

Safeguard your assets with silver:

Silver and gold tend to be closely related to each other; when the value of gold upsurges on account of monetary ambiguity, fiscal breakdowns, insurgency, and political improbability, silver is guaranteed to progress at the same rate as gold. This is because valuable metals are inclined to be associated with each other. Although this association is not essentially mandatory, yet the cost of silver coins escalates as soon as the value of low grade silver or silver bars ape up (due to ambiguity in the market.) This is an illustrious factor because gold has a tendency to escalate mechanically when there is a great deal of financial and civic insecurity. Silver is likely to belly up with the approval of gold.

There are also several other justifications why the worth of silver increases unremittingly.

1. *Silver coins have their own savings worth:*

Silver as a metal is a chronological stock up of worth. Even if employed for commerce or for ornaments, silver churns out as an investment with intrinsic value such as oil, natural gas, gold, and land used for farming and to lesser grade industrial properties. By and large most hard bargains are an outstanding investment that will in general escalate in worth all through the phases of more than median price hikes. For example gold serves as an inflation hedge or a hard asset for the reason that it predictably increases in worth all through periods of inflation. Resources that are utilized to obstruct against price hike are generally unhelpfully allied with shares of stocks and bonds. During phases of towering price hike, stocks and bonds are liable to deteriorate, while investments with intrinsic value e.g. silver, gold, oil, natural gas etc are likely to do better.

Price hike has been scratching in height in the preceding years; therefore it should be no amazement to understand that resources like silver, gold, oil have functioned extraordinarily all through those times.

Putting forth, surplus sum of assets in accounts giving a low return is disastrous all through phases of price hike, seeing that your capital is mislaying usefulness very swiftly (soaring price hike signifies that the purchasing strength of cash dwindles). That's the reason folks prefer to have possession of savings that are thought to offer defense against the declining significance of a currency (so as to look after their total assets) since it has an immense genuine worth. Having said that, you amplify your probabilities of earning capital with silver by purchasing silver coins.

How?

Silver coins possess their individual genuine worth. That's correct. Silver coins fetch a cumulative worth. Not only would folks desire to purchase silver coins owing to the base silver metal substance that they possess but for the reason that the value of silver coins increases with time. As well as similar to any aggregate entries, the more precious an article is, the more high-priced it becomes; this modus operandi holds valid for silver coins. As a matter of fact, ancient silver coins exceed in value on the footing of mass in comparison the base metal that it holds. When you endow in silver coins, you are actually involved in a bifurcated asset approach:

- You are funding in the random worth of the valuable metal

- You are funding in the cumulative worth of silver coins

Therefore, you acquire two courses of worth by funding in silver coins.

2. *Silver is a savings refuge during monetary catastrophe:*

As soon as folks begin becoming distressed about the strength of the financial system, or they become nervous owing to economic volatility, they throng to valued metals such as silver in a brief time, with slight/no trouncing in worth. The latter are among the assets that can be converted into cash; you can effortlessly vend silver or gold in the market. In addition, they are mighty stock piles of worth as paper money mislays its cost and as constitutional administrations turn up and leave, public reliance on valuable metals stays the same. Given that they are very straightforward to exchange and their worth stays for a long period of time; silver pulls out as an immense asset asylum all through monetary disasters. As acknowledged earlier, silver coins put in an additional stratum of worth for the reason that silver coins are also collectables. Consequently not only do you acquire more worth from your pool of silver coins in the course of a financial breakdown, but you can also trade them very promptly equally for:

- The collectors' worth reward
- The worth of the base metal they enclose

3. *Ease of access of silver is its crucial power:*

An ultimate crucial operator for the cost of silver and silver's ability to recover readily all through monetarily difficult times is the reality that it is easy to get to. Dissimilar to gold which can be quite costly measured up to silver, the latter is much economical. As a consequence, more public would want to throng into silver. This can affect (on a proportional source) a towering degree of approval and admiration in comparison to gold. Since gold is more difficult to get to (owing to its cost) it is trouble-free to jaunt percentage price instability with silver. To put it in another way, you get more return for your investment with silver since it is more easily reached. The negative aspect to endowing in silver coins and silver as a whole is that it is so within reach that if there is a sudden increase in price, public might move to the market with their serving spoons of silver, ornaments of silver and industrialized silver. This is what came about in the eighties when gamblers attempted to buy up all the viable companies vending silver (so as to have power over the price at which it was put up for sale).

4. *Pull out induction:*

While purchasing silver in bulk in the form of rounds, coins, or bars, there are a few aspects to be considered prior to deciding on. In case you are concerned about syndicating your pull out into valuable metals, you ought to use a silver IRA------ an investment.

Silver Bullion is stocks certificates of now days!

With the monetary world influencing from one net income per share to a different, there has been an abrupt surge in small scale shareholders, who would preferably pay money for silver bullion than assets or commodities which would go up today to go down in the future. Contribution in this proposes more monetary protection than a contribution in certificates of debt/glimmering dividends. Despite the fact that all these modes of monetary tools functioned pretty well and the shareholders obtained enormous remuneration in the seventies and the eighties, it is not the situation these days.

The monetary markets across the world are self-supporting; therefore this mode of venture is the most reliable and protected preference for all and sundry. The chances of buying stock in silver reserves are scarce.

As silver bars can be purchased and operated in numerous shapes and categories, it calls for an astute depositor to interpret the market drifts and select the right variety of silver bars which will fetch him the highest profits. Silver ingots are bought and sold in huge amounts on the swap over of commodities. The costs at which this is purchased and put on the market is no more than pinpointing because the tangible market worth for the smaller quantity (that the minor investor operates in) is very irrelevant. That's why the cost of the one troy ounce silver coin (which is 0.999 genuine) considerably goes beyond the trifling cost of one ingot silver biscuit (which is 0.999 genuine). One more feature to be contemplated with silver bullion is that, given the suitable forms in which it is offered, the small time depositor would rather change the whole of his cash on hand, in these periods of challenge and stress; where the price of a share (or an unprotected loan certificate given out by a corporation, supported by general credit instead of particular assets) is not proficient to obtain the value of the paper it is published on. If a depositor were to mistakenly select the form, he is never at jeopardy for the reason that; the worth of silver will stay the same, no matter what form it turns up.

A lot has been alleged about this selection since it is the long-established form of venture all across the globe. Antique societies and civilizations have numerous customs and mores related with the silver ingots of those days, regardless of whether it was the silver ingot or the rudimentary silver penny.

The reason for putting up dough in Silver Bullion

It is often said that during troubling times people flock back to traditional values. In the financial world flocking back to traditional values means a return to the precious metals. In the highly volatile times we live in, traditionally strong currencies such as the U.S. dollar and the British Pound are quickly losing value. The pound has lost up to 30% of its value against other currencies like the yen in the last year. Likewise despite the USD at first being upheld at the crisis point by a rush into U.S. treasury bonds, this temporary upswing has now been reversed as fundamentals push down the USD against other currencies. As the United States attempts to print its way out of recession giving bankrupt banks vast amounts of tax payer money to attempt to stop a financial collapse even the average citizen fears what is about to come next. For history teaching us once those printing presses start rolling inflation and even hyper inflation is on the way. Unemployment and associated problems only increase the panic.

People want to move into something that will protect their underlying wealth, or even ensure they have something, anything that they can trade. Therefore they move into resources that will not lose value. Gold has been the traditional hedge in such times, but it does not take long for the price to be prohibitive as it is a rare resource. Most Gold is held by the large investors leaving little for the small investor to get at a reasonable price. There is however another precious metal that is more easily available to the small investor - it is silver, and currently it is relatively cheap to Gold with a 1:70 ratio. This ratio has no sensible explanation given that the ratio they are found in the earth is about 1:13.5. Should silver return to its God given ratio - those holding silver are likely to become very rich.

Silver has many qualities and properties that make it a very useful industrial commodity. For example silver paste is used in 90% of solar cells - and with many predicting and even demanding the move to renewable energy, the demand for solar panels is predicted to skyrocket. Thus the demand for silver paste is correspondingly over to increase. But if one takes a detailed look at just how many industrial processes silver is involved in - its demand just as a commodity has the potential to skyrocket. But many are seeing that the real increase in the price of silver will be the demand for it as an investment.

Silver is molded into bullion bars and coins. As such it forms an easily transportable form of wealth. Each bar is marked with its purity and weight and normally a makers mark. If you want to see how easily these items are traded one can check on eBay and see that bullion is highly tradable and convertible into cash.

As cash continues to lose its value, silver underlying value will increase in proportion. (For example if you had left your money in the bank last year you would have seen a low interest return (3%-5%) on which you would be required to pay tax. In truth by sitting your money in the bank you are losing value when inflation is factored in. If you had put the money into silver you could have seen a 56% increase in value). But where investors see the real increase in the demand for silver will be the demand to have something other than paper with which to trade, buy and sell. Once this process again becomes accepted to the general public the value of silver will only increase further.

The only way I see silver not exploding in value would be if some massive silver mine was discovered - I mean massive in the sense of billions of ounces. This happened when the "new world" was discover in the 1500's, but I very much doubt that with the world now explored there is another silver el Dorado not yet found. Currently silver mining production is about 600 million ounces most of which is currently used and "consumed" meaning any sizable move into silver as bullion will greatly increase its price. There simply isn't as much silver around as there once was.

The fundamental law of supply and demand is very well known. It is a law that is beginning to be applied to silver with people realizing it is a finite resource, it is precious.

Why invest in Silver bullion? To make money on an increasingly limited and in demand resource. By having physical possession of Silver in bullion form you know you actually have it, in precise quantity and quality and not just a paper promise.

On a silver platter!

The apprehension of price hike has got millions of financiers striving for reliable investment choices for their capital in comparison to what they had formerly been utilizing. Lots of investment and monetary counselors are counting on silver as an approach to defend their depositor's money from the awful effects of price hike that is unavoidable. Analogous private business authorities are relatively forceful in their prop up of the long duration investments in silver as a guard against the forthcoming price hike that monetary counselors have been mentioned as declaring what they had contemplated would start to emerge in the subsequent two to five years. Silver continues to be one of the most indispensable valuable metals across the globe.

Silver has a whole host of uses.

Despite the fact that gold may be the most accepted of the valuable metals, it is used more or less utterly for ornaments and beautification functions, while silver on the contrary is extensively used. Owing to its significance to the knowledge manufactory as an essential constituent of numerous electronic gadgets such as cell phones, TV sets etc. Silver is distinctively perched to amplify very much in value in the approaching years. In reality, some market forecasters probe whether or not the worth of silver has not been kept falsely low for the last many years.

*V*alue of silver will ultimately ape up, buy silver right away!

Investing in silver bullion is far less costly than gold, though the low availability and the ever-increasing demand on the existing supply (due to the high use in technological applications) will no doubt raise the price of silver in the coming years. The trend toward investment in precious metals is growing in popularity as larger numbers of people are becoming disheartened by their failing investments in the stock market and other traditional methods of investing.

Why Silver coins can save your ass in the forthcoming times?

You have to be familiar with the fact that "*anything that has risen must eventually fall down.*" This is out-and-out with the force of attraction; not only is this fair with the material world but is unquestionably true with pecuniary merchandising; you don't have to be a mastermind to think this through. When you analyze the NASDAQ all through its entire life span, you would make out crucial prototype where the total market escalates then it adjusts itself. Although the sureness of market adjustments is a forceful dramatic move, the promptness of such alterations is astute. If folks are able to calculate when the market is going to rectify itself, then the market would be overflowing with big shots. The reality is no one makes out, and this is exactly the reason for the stock market to be so rewarding. In any case, with endless threats, you acquire immeasurable dividends. The encouraging information is that you need not participate in the market completely unguarded. By endowing in expensive metals such as silver coins, you can guarantee that no matter what correction the market experiences, you would be in an absolutely reliable position. Keep in mind that as far as market correction is concerned, your monetary strength is proportional. If you believe you've mislaid some of your resources, even then regard yourself fortunate. If you judge yourself against others who misplaced it all, it's truly all comparative. By placing your resources in such a manner, you can truly gain from market adjustments (when stocks are affected there is a constructive outcome on how lofty silver will finish up progressing). There are specific ventures you can latch onto that not only assist you endure astute descents in the market but can also place you in such a manner that you are able to churn out money on account of such descents. Silver coins endow with such safeguard.

*F*inest choices of silver investments:

Most of you might not be aware of the fact that by purchasing silver coins, you are placing yourself to mint quite a reasonable amount of money at a time when there is a sudden decline of stock prices across a noteworthy cross-section of the stock market. This could be done by transforming your *Individual Retirement Account* (essentially a savings account with immense tax concessions, making it just the right way to stock away money for the period when you sit in your rocker and look at the fire) or your *401k retirement plan* into silver assets and your free investments into silver coins, you effectively come up with a hedge when the market slides down. As soon as the market breaks down, you can relocate a few of your silver possessions into ready cash. Later, you can employ this ready cash coupled with the fringe that you get from your adviser to quickly get a great deal of stagnant shares of colossal companies (with solid reputations.) Generally the market goes through a swift move up subsequent to a crucial smash. You can then egress your margin positions when you get a swift jack up and then hold on to some of your shares of very huge and well systematized companies as takings. By gradually moving up and down subsequent to a sudden dramatic decline of stock prices; utilizing the level to which a market permits assets (such as silver coins) to be bought and sold at stable prices, you can truly achieve.

Every cloud has a silver lining!

Though in no way it is evident where the costs of things will proceed; nonetheless silver is even now a canny and intelligent manner to evade price hike and pay attention to your investments protecting it from a possible break down of the market. Even apportioning a slight fraction of your personal account into silver will endow you with a defense against prospective sudden dramatic decline in stock prices. Don't overlook to appreciate that spending in costly metals such as silver not only assists you in battling against stinging deteriorations in the market, but also assists you in ranking yourself to gain benefits from market resumptions. At the absolute minimum, putting up dough in silver assists you to convert your assets to ready money whenever you need a resource. Silver has its benefits and should be taken into account for anybody's personal account.

Even if you are waiting to:

- Procure phenomenal silver coinage
- Endow in silver with a stockbroker

Both the aforementioned choices are illustrious and should be reflected on.

Get Physical Silver now!

www.ingramcontent.com/pod-product-compliance
Lightning Source LLC
Chambersburg PA
CBHW071206220526
45468CB00002B/507